SPARE

In loving memory of my dear friends:

John Demar
Carolyn Gilliland

SPARE

a poetic memoir

Reese Taylor

PREFACE

Loss was a primary propeller, which kicked up old loves in the dust. Through writing I framed the ache—the pain of losing my beloved and his brothers, then surfaced the deaths of my brother, my father, mother, and my two best friends. In this landslide of loss I found memories and emotions swirling around my body. When I recall all of this the icon of corpse pose warrants a click.

I wrote in spits and spurts. Poems woke me up in the night. They spoke in rage and anger and sometimes served as a kiss goodnight. Descriptors of feelings real and sometimes unattractive began to spell my name. Victim, hungry, cynic, joker salved the pain. In between those brutal bruises love continued to peek through. I could not ignore what spilled out of my heart, my hand. Love is as real as rage and I held them both. One is easier to hold on its own than the endless juggle. I walked, got out of bed and held you in my breath.

And so I wrote until the subject weaned itself from me. The tone changed over time. With that shift, I knew that this book was complete. The love I feel for the people who stirred these emotions is still present and their place is held within me.

I feel grateful for the power of the creative process. I hope that the awesome transitions that I have experienced through this work will speak to you, the reader, in ways that feel real.

to the Beloved

After a While

After a while you learn
to bring expectations into the cabin of your own heart
to feed chambers of cravings, offering apricots to the gods
to notice when grace visits and hands out wildflower bouquets
to keep time with mockingbirds who sing again in June
to speak and pray in private, to own wisdom as yours
to flip surety upside down and give dreams a different form
to accept and to wish in unison
and then be on your way.

After a while you learn . . .
that regardless, chaos turns to plans
seldom written in your own hand

In the Beginning

Can I make you dinner?
Okay
Fear snaked in
Salmon on the patio
Fed
Bright eyes

Phone calls
Conversation
Pluto
Rotating on its side
Spread
Magnetic energy
Like glitter
Sprinkled
Over candlelight

Wives and husbands,
Reviewed
Movies and a touch
Of your hand
In mine
Feelings expand

Six weeks imbibing
In the mystery
Soaking in fantasies
Resulted
In a party for two
Danced
In the living room
Dipped
In the hot tub
Your kiss
Insane
Moonrise
Sealed the deal

Adventures
Followed
Compassion and passion
Beers and prayers
A ride in your car
Camping
Under heaven
Peace
Settled in

Life
Threw rocks
Instead of curve balls
We
Caught them
And threw them back
Into the walls
Of Diablo canyon
Naked
We danced

Half a dozen
Deaths
Interrupted
Happiness
Pinches of fear
Swelled
Through our bliss
Until closeness
Turned silent

Pagan pain
Closed doors
Locked love
In lonely
Memory
Of me
With you
Naked
We danced.

Pissing on God's Campfire

Cut my chest open
Pry my ribs apart
like a hunter gutting a deer

The A-line drips
A hose in my throat chokes me as nurses say: Relax
Machines keep time with body rhythms,
chemistry and flashing lights
So many monitors that the room turns musical
                              As I doze and puke
                                 doze and puke

My girlfriend slips my iPod headphones into my ears
She hits play, holds my hand and
stares at my frog-positioned legs
She prays that fluids from my body drain

Prays that the respirator can be removed
That a repeated surgical repair won't be my next trip

I just want her to go away
She's there and there and there
Guilt grabs my recovery
I want to pull her hair.

Where's my son
He'll help me
Be there for me
Like I've been there for him

God, I want a cigarette
Piss in a tube
Morphine on a button
Charts and sitting nurses
and her, she's still there

Waking up more and more
Day one, day two, day three
Relief reflects in faces of friends
Ice chips turn to Jello
Is this the end?

No—out of CCU they wheel me
My five star room becomes a two
Accidents from a snowstorm take my nurses
Regret racks me—God why did I agree to this?
Cuts on my heart feel untended
My artificial valve clicks time

She sleeps on the floor beside me
I hate being in this bed
My son drives me home
She carries my stuff…
oxygen and a pill schedule there for me

My dirty gown days give way to
clean sheets, the cats and home
She showers me and washes my hair
My strength allows me to sit
Let her do it, clean me
dress my wound
pull me up and help me down

Down onto a half dozen pillows she carefully arranged
so my chest doesn't feel like it will crack
Sleep and oxygen, movies and my son beside me
She defers to the other room

What's wrong with her?
Why does she stay with me?
Go away
Leave me alone
My son will take care of me

I will take care of me

Warmed by a fire I walk
First five minutes, then ten
She urges gently, tries so hard to stay my lover
while my recovery forces her to be my mother
She takes really good care of me.

I love her and I don't want her
It hurts too much to need anyone
I need a cigarette
Can't I just have one cigarette?
Then I'll quit, I'll be good.

She feeds me and cheers me
Urges me to walk, then rest
She climbs on the roof to dust the snow
from the satellite dish so I won't go crazy
Who else would do this for me?

Who else could see through me?

My son leaves after Christmas
We have two feet of snow
pushing us together like a snowman
There's nowhere to go

I cried like a baby when my son left.
Why?
A big burst of sobbing brought
her soft kiss to my cheek
then privacy to let it rip.

She's still there in the atmosphere
Though I try to ignore her
as friends come and go
Christmas visits, food and wines
Cheerful sights. I gain my strength

She helps me into the cars of friends
Or she drives me where I need to go
Go faster, park here, no there
I criticize as my strength begins to grow.

Two months pass
A red zipper and two dots mar my chest
She rubs oils lightly so the color can fade
Maybe no one will know.

Maybe no one will know
That she's still here and how much she helped me
And now how I want her to go
I make her wrong and fat or bitchy
Anything but the truth

Can't she just get up and go

I can drive now
Drive away from her
Leave her on the brink
She'll figure it out I say
When I leave her out
When I go out to play

Finally, I say it
Go away, I want to be alone
She cried like they all do
Next day the closet looms, emptied
Maybe I made a mistake

No…she did
She walked back in
needing me
NO, I need me
Get out I roar
She goes and goes

Comes back and goes

I erect fences
Then mountains
And she's still there

I treat my repaired heart
to a cigarette,
then two, now three
beers, new women
mean messages I send

She's over there now
and she's still here.

Igloo of Eternity

Memories form an avalanche
Bones begin to roll
Heartbreak overwhelms me
Clamps of icy crystals
Chill the pain
Enclosed

In an igloo of eternity
Breath begins to slow
Mind and muscles give in
Till mourning rests
My body takes a deep breath
As white light begins to flow

Golden beams join a presence
Heavy darkness dims
Knowing and rejoicing
This journey soon will end

The next life seeks me
Garden paths expand
Lying in your essence
I feel
The pressure of
Your hand.

Power to Create

Miracles are based in love, not fear
says a line that invites study once more
Gratitude flows and washes the soul
like a warm bath filled with lilies

So how does love stick without glue
to the bends of my brain,
the chambers of my heart?

Painting, writing, relationships
come forward and go away
staccato, allegro, notes on the page,
current chapters of life.

Friends see talents and encourage
paint the first stroke, strike a note,
print a page, hang a shingle.

Internally, I sigh and roll my eyes
certain they are just being nice
and drone on about my lack
of computer skills, a flat stomach
or some misplaced judgment
from my mind's eye.

How does the pump prime enough
to power critical mass,
to propel transition time forward,
to create a tangible end?

Spare

One

Write me a poem that's spare —
Few words, cut and clean
With a message aimed with precision
Into the depths of the heart
Into the mechanics of the aortic valve
That clicks like a skeleton watch
Works like Apollo coming home
To earth through a very narrow window
One movement
To a single degree
Left or right
Makes the whole thing
Work perfectly
Precisely, with room to spare.

Two

Can you offer a word or two
A hug, a kiss to wish me well
Without breaking in two

Your Mother's Day greeting
Addressed to me…and twenty more
Is indeed,
Spare.

My thoughts went toward your mother
Who had so little of her own self
That her offerings to her little boy
Were clammy and clingy

Pressed against her red nightgown
You served her well,
A spare husband
Then an extra wheel
When Dad and Mom fell apart

Three

The words flow down
Between red boulders
Of the Rocky mountains
A waterfall in spring
Flying beside two bodies
Hugging the mass
Standing on a rock shelf
In the spray from torrents of water
Without an inch to spare.

Four

Crouched in a window seat
On an old airplane headed for Paris
Listening to bedroom music
Recorded by you
My emotions hold hands
They cannot move

Love flows
Like pink ruffles
Cascading over breasts
Cornered,
Cast in armor
Protecting truth

I want you there
To show me Lyon
As sunlight fades over grapevines
Before we catch the bullet train
Toward the city of lights
Without any time to spare.

Five

Spare me another year
Of heartache my love
Open your wings
And shed the burdens
Of your ancestors
As I peal away
The cloisters of mine
Dance in the river
Dive under the dam
Swimming up,
Renewed

Hours in flight
Turn to minutes
Will I see you there?
Blooming
Spring and autumn
Watered by winter's snow
Melting from your kiss
Breathing again
In your arms
Wading in the moonlight
Quivering through the night
Of a lifetime

Do you have one to spare?

He recounts

Let go
Dear heart
Do not love me.

Near or far
Turn away
Then burn me.

Let me stay
In silent hate
With sin's soft hands
Around my skin
Do not tell me.

Bring me loneliness
On a tray that I deserve
Pierced with nails
For the hearts I bruised
And mangled.

Let me lie
In my own quiet cell
Take your kiss away
It stings me.

Tears etch rivers
Filling pools that deliver
The message
That you adore me.

Angry howling muffles
My love's whispers
Do not move toward me.

When your brother dies

I had a brother that died. Well, more than one really. But a biological brother that died. He was almost five and I was almost three. He was a Taurus, like me. I guess he was earthy, like me. He died eight days before my third birthday. He died four days before Easter that year. Apparently he was buried on Friday and by Sunday my mother dressed us up in our Easter outfits and we marched down the isle of the Methodist church and took a seat in the pew. I bet my daddy skipped that Sunday. He probably went to his shop and had a drink or two. We sat through a service I'm sure I don't remember since I don't remember that little boy.

My mother told me forty years later that he used to push me around in a box over the polished wooden floors. He laughed because I did in my babyish gurgle. He wore cowboy clothes and a gun on a belt. He was western the way little boys were in the 50s. No one at home ever talked about him but there was a beautiful picture of the blond, blue-eyed little boy next to the portrait of me with my brown-eyed sister. I didn't know when his birthday was or the day that he died until I was a grown girl. Only then did I know why I was so depressed for every one of my birthdays. He died and then I blew out my candles and the two incidents were braided into death for me. I couldn't separate him from me. No one spoke of him or me. My mother went to bed until she could get up and steel herself against the pain, until she could cook the meals and pay the bills and bury her boy. Daddy went to Denver, to work until he came back. Sometimes, he just stayed away.

The Oklahoma City bombing happened two days before my birthday after decades of time had passed. My brother was only a picture until the news flashed of the bombing and a nine story building collapsing on a bunch of people including a preschool filled with little boys and little girls and I flew to pieces. My adult and child self collided into a reality frozen long ago. I didn't understand it but I knew it and my world began to explode. Fear of annihilation kept me awake at night while survivor's guilt plagued my days. Powerlessness was no longer an AA slogan. It was right up against my face. Grief took on a sound, a pagan sound that reverberated for weeks as my cells began to buckle. Tears couldn't explain why this pain had been ingrained in my memory. A bombing brought my baby girl self alive with the loss of my "big" brother. Rocking myself out of the box that held my memory of him, a rhythm of him as he pushed me around the room. With his gun on his belt, he pushed me around the room.

The Centaur

You cross the ocean
Bearing the bridle of death
So sure as the metal
Pinching your teeth
You won't return again

Pull the wagon
Across the sea
Delivering your beloved
To the doorstep of her dream
A voyage for new life
Hauling a payload of latitude
To truly be heroic
To only be herself

You brush your soft coat
And whinny well wishes
Over and again
While the fog cools
Your shimmering skin
The muted moon spooks you—
Like Beowulf
Keen ears perk up
Hearing remnants of songs
You sing in Old English
She chants
In a land of fresh hay
In a land of overcast days

Dreams of blue sky tug at you
Dreams of bulbous white clouds
A bridge spanning the great gorge
Your hoofs tap out a dance
A prance step, a time step
Flickers of imagination
Nostrils flare

You trot around her
Showing your teeth
Flashing adoration
For her journey so steep

She feeds you oats and carrots
Brings blankets to cover your back
But now you've sprouted wings
Half horse, half man
With feathered wings
In between

And so you fly
With a kiss goodbye
Heading west
You fly like Pegasus
Flying so fast
Chasing your quest

Bridle turns to garland
You begin to race
Spirit guides from the Lakota
Jockey you to this place
Where cottonwoods glisten
In fall's gentle sun
Where air smells of pinon
And swells inside your lungs
Here turquoise doorways open
Hawks fly above your head

Shucking your saddle
You choose a dressage
Jumping barrels and fences
Clearing passion and joy
Galloping and cantering
More minutes surround you
With a coin tossed for luck
You win your own race

Lush green grass
Carpets the winner's circle
Cushions hot hooves
From tests and time trials
In the grandstands
Applause explodes
They adore you.

Cheers
Rise up meeting
Your luminous eyes
Pleasure
Barely contained
As a thousand tiny red roses
Cover all that remains

Your head nods
In exalted wonder
Knowing,
Through miles and strides
Man or beast
There is no disgrace

For today, in this ring
You win first place.

Pride and Confidence

Get up, put your panties on
Wrap a push up bra around your chest
Just for effect

A skirt, a shirt
Grass green summer sandals
That should do

Walk into a salon
For someone else to wash your hair
Paint your toenails

Julia Roberts sunglasses
Should hide your eyes
The façade begins

Go to the bank
Get some twenties
And a hundred too
Armed for the ride

Stand up tall and straight
Prop three days in bed
Into some sort of vertical stance

Find some endorphins
Find them fast
Glue them on like cottonballs

Make it quick
Before you run into someone
Who can topple this dance
With a flick of an eye

Put on your high heels
And your red satin dress
Let your shattered psyche
Rest & rest & rest

Pride and confidence
Born not raised?
Decades old baby steps
Just can't keep pace

Existential Ballet

Standing still
In the heat of a spotlight
Shining realizations burn
Efforts to hang on
To our skin

Wonder if there's time
For an elegant developé
Like a dancer standing on point
Slowly raising foot to knee
Then extending a leg out
Into the world
Committing to
A tiny toe point
Of balance
From earth to air

Can we consolidate
Into confidence
With a dancer's grace
Into all that we are
Emerging without falling back
Into the gloom
Into the womb
Into shackles of survival
Patterns thrown behind us

Heroic echoes guide us
Right and left
Notes of encouragement
To lift up
Hold hands
To live, renewed
Without review

From every line *

From every line there peers out at me
a force that wants to see me win

Force cheers wildly in the wings
makes supper and presses my clothes

Force drives me toward committed pages
"Good line, nice metaphor," Force insists.

Steadfast presence burns urgently,
wills me there once more

"Please, please me," says Force
And pen meets paper again..

Living on the Point of my Finger

Hey you, you over there
Who do you think you are?
Pointing your hate this way
Rejecting kindness
Offering coldness
Isn't there a better way?

Projected attitudes sting with assaults
Painful lives loop into themselves
Judgments and insults about yourself
Fly across my face

Calmly I stand, smiling,
Loving you anyway
Until built up rage finally blows
Bleeding out of the side of my neck

Blasting away first quiet, then loud
Hating you boomerangs around
To hating myself
The cycle begins again

Love breeds love
Until fear scares closeness
Into closeted silence
Connection denied

Hey you, you over there
Who do you think you are?
Loving me so courageously
Holding my life compassionately
Masking the message: You suck

Stay with your reality
Breathe anger in, then out
Wrap your arms around me
Around yourself
Brilliance beams at last

Living on the point of my finger
Reflects truth about the pointer
Turn around
Turn it around
Around, around & around.

Regardless

I love you
It does not matter
What you think
Or do

Years expand
Dreams regress
But love beats
Steady
Within my chest

I love you
Regardless
Of me
And you

You wax
I wane
Moonlight shines
On love's remains

Gardening for Life

Yesterday, I gardened all day. It was hot but I managed well by seeking shade. I continue landscaping a beautiful house on the hill. My work is my baby, my craft. The house belongs to him. He has a crew with tools and muscles. I work alone. He builds a deck, installs a moss-laden rock fountain and builds a trail down the 30° slope of his land, complete with switchbacks. The house belongs to him, the yard is mine. Our fingerprints are tattooed all over our respective venues. Love cruises like a protective cloud, hovering, with wings. I plant thyme in the spaces between flagstones and in those spaces my life makes sense.

In the afternoon I moved my parched self across town to the west side. My friend of thirty years lived in this old New Mexican cottage until April 23rd when he took a gun to himself in the ultimate search for peace. He left this great old property to his ex-wife, a present reflecting love that moved through time like a mountain stream. Through France to Santa Fe he carried a love for her that wouldn't go away. She lives in Fayetteville and needs some help keeping the weeds at bay—so here I go gardening for a dead man and his ex in the fullness of July sun.

I bought a honeysuckle to soften the front porch and sweeten the fragrance for those who come to sit in his old wicker chair, smoke a cigarette and cry for him. Cry for the friend that we lost and for the fact that we could not save him. I pulled the careless weeds and trimmed the thorny pyrocanthia under the felt sense of his watchful eyes. I had wanted to tame these grounds for the past few years and yesterday I found myself wondering, "Why?" and "Why didn't I?" Would our shared loneliness have found a place to reside as it turned over again and again into the ground, transformed into the potential of a poppy or a rose? Could shared purpose have stopped the bullet from taking air from his nose? Now, he is gone, my *brother*, my friend and I dig and dig, scrape leaves from sand with my hands, trying to straighten up, attempting to turn tears into beauty, grief into oxygen, as I mulch this ground, I know I'm gardening for life.

Last Night *

Last night as I was sleeping
I heard the two screaming natives outside
turning each other into one big blue bruise

I vowed to block their violence
flipping on a fan oscillating peace and brilliance
into my mind like a dance

I dreamed Benitio del Toro took me
into his strong, bronze arms across continents
into moonlight mist where nothing ever fails

I saw myself emerging
from a pool of iridescent waters
a faery with my own burning wand

Last night as I was sleeping
I imagined my white veiled marriage to God
King of the spirit world
Queen of the wild
Guardian of Souls

I never wanted to awaken
the fear mongers who often crowd my days
My breath blew the winds that were true
A baby, a woman, a crone
All three came visiting

My dreams came too
spirit soothed
each night my soul
appeared renewed

A flute sang a lullaby as I shut my eyes
Closed the door to all chaos—gone, removed.
A spirit entered the bedroom to cradle me gently
Last night as I was sleeping

Seduction Waltz

The way you use her
The way you schmooze her
To certify what happens
inside your pants

The way you use her
The way you schmooze her
While denial clouds your
creation of the dance

The way you use her
The way you schmooze her
As satisfaction creeps
up your spine to advance

You dream of a honeymoon
In her living room
And your ego takes a chance

Through meandering poetry
You both begin to prance...
Prance, dance, chance
Sneak, peak, blink
Waltz around your vows

Alert your mind
Remember what's thine
Reflected visions of your ring
wipe out the trance

The fog frames clear
As she cries in your mirror
While you deny the way you use her
The way you schmooze her

Then drop her on her ass.

After Ecclesiastes 3:107

Sunday night I slept in my mother's isolation room at the hospital. She looked like pink parchment paper. She didn't really look sick but her energy was not there. The tests for a form of TB were still outstanding but I didn't care. I was intent upon being there when her cardiologist made his Monday morning rounds. I spoon fed my mother, washed her face, brushed her teeth, her hair. She smiled when I helped her, accepting these basic small acts.

Maybe I was no longer too much to bear.

Dr. Chappell met my sister and me in the hall to give us the expected but dreaded news. He said "infection" and "resistant" and "Hospice" in the same sentence.

It felt like launching a balloon into a vacuum.

We returned to our mother's room. I sat on one side of the bed, my sister sat on the other. I took my mother's hand.

I hadn't held her hand before, except to cross the street.

Dr. Chappell applauded mother for being such a good patient and doing everything he said to do . . . "but even though she had put up a good fight the bacterial infection in her lungs was winning and it was going to win . . . it was going to take her life."

She squeezed my hand as she looked the doctor in the eye and resolutely said, "Okay."

She began to sing an unfamiliar hymn in her warbled voice, something about finding peace in the Promised Land. Her doctor stood honorably listening to all three verses before he left the room. That day there was time to usher in the beginning of the end.

Oh my God, Run, he said.

(to be read as fast as possible)

Oh shit
there she is

What do I do
Where can I go?

Feel the anxiety
I'm okay

Gulp it down
no one knows

Look around
Oh good, no one knows

Oh God
she's coming near

Pretend,
the usual

Kiss, kiss
Hello

Oh no
it didn't work

Kiss, kiss on the cheek
landed on her lips

Oh fuck
now what?

How are you?
Perfect, she says

Perfect?
really?

She's perfect.
And you? she asks

I'm good
(or some equivalent salutation)

Great!
she says walking away

Looking at her
I wink

I winked
What made me wink?

Oh God
I winked

Now what?
32 weeks of iron clad ignoring
just got shot in the ass

I winked
I kissed her on the lips

Okay, rub against the blonde
quick-go fast

Stick a beer
in my pocket

Tease the blonde
go outside

Smoke a cigarette
suck it up

Walk back in
pretend

I'm the real deal
the one with a surface crack

No one sees it
do they?

Walk out
no go back in

The crack doesn't show
Oh no!

Go back in.

Okay, I'll Go, she said

Okay, I'll go to the party
I pick up my friends
My red car up the road
toward the birthday bash

My estranged lover's truck is there
The truck, with a headache rack
which matches his Jack Nicholson eyebrows

Oh boy, no, oh shit, he's there
Bets are made on how fast he will run
out of the house once he sees me there

5 minutes, 5 seconds, 10, no two.

I'm dressed like a Russian
in tall black boots
and a black fitted sweater
hugging a shiny brown Nicole Miller skirt
my attitude veering toward France

Fresh cut bangs
not too much make-up
a little slimmer, tighter
I place my smile and walk in

He's the first person I see
Oh God — he's the first person I see

I'm cool
Hello, hello to the host
Happy Birthday
I brought you a bottle of wine

I'm gliding with my smile
in my boots and my shiny skirt
Pretending to be a princess
I reach his side to say, hello

A kiss
He winks as I back away
a vibrational override
to weeks of ignoring

He moves toward a blonde in a leather jacket
the one who leans into him
someone explains that
she's his new main squeeze

He moves in jerks
smokes a cigarette outside
comes back in
goes out again

After hours at the party
Finally, we leave.
He, follows friends out the door
sees me and stops in his tracks
like playing mother may I?

Stop, hold tight
On the square
under my own feet
All I can do is stare

I can't say two steps forward
Only one back
Now I play the game
Knowing
I must step inside.

I don't know anything

I realize more and more that I don't know anything. I don't know how to be with him and he doesn't know how to be with me. I feel like I'm cracking up.

I saw myself as the enlightened one and him as the identified patient. Now I know that is not true. I'm further down the path of understanding how life effects everyone from birth forward but I do not know how to be in a relationship any more than he does. I cry over this ignorance and the damage it has done and I hold my ignorance as if it might be a geode, which could crack open under the pressure of pain and reveal purple prisms of a new reality.

I've held this hard round ball of rock in my personal backpack for years. I've taken it out and wondered about it, sometimes out-loud regarding its' meaning, and put it back. The weight of it remains.

I want someone else to crack it and deliver the purple crystals to my door wrapped in silver tissue paper in a heavy paper sack with handles, but that's not the way it works.

Doing my own sit-ups makes my abdomen flat.
Reading my selection of material increases my knowledge and inspiration.
Taking my own steps forward does exactly that—moves me forward.

To what end? Alone? With God or Buddha? To stay or to go? All of the answers complete the circle entitled—
I DO NOT KNOW.

Oprah Winfrey has a section in her magazine titled,
"What I know for sure" consisting of various essays of a
positive flavor documenting the essence of some sure
thing. I don't know what I would write in that column.
Maybe I would write that I'm breathing this morning
and I cried last night and today and that I'm not sure
why or why now?

The geode has a crack in it and my backpack has a hole
in it and I don't know what to do.

Take a bath and put on your clothes. That seems real.

Buddhist Riddle

What is this
        is that
What is not this
        is not that

No, no
Not this
not that
Just this
and that

That this
this that
Yes to this
        and yes to that

This, that
not this, not that

It spins and spins
        into this
        or is it that?

Icon

I have a new icon to help me through
A shiny car with a pig-headed hood ornament
Great paint job and cushy leather seats
which eject the passenger upon command

The spark plugs fire
the engine mostly works
but the transmission is screwed

Drive works from time to time
until steaming neutral takes over
And then there's reverse

Reverse is the worst

Reverse happens without warning
seamless, no grinding
it clicks in and then
all other gears are gone

Just gone

Daddy—Pull the Plug, 1985

Break the ribs
Open up
Connect the tubes
Turn on the pump

Check the pressure
Connect the tack
Remove the clots
Scrape the frack

Stroke, strike one
Crash, strike two
Sinus rhythm, hang three
Brain dead, who knew

Surgical maniacs
Prescribed the power
Of a well-lived life
30,000 dollars toward
a vegetable of you

Yes ma'am,
Your husband is alive
Plugged into eternity
You can see him through
Her counted cross-stitch blurred

Ashen skin
He beats again
Death knocks
Between the doors

Residual bliss
Retroactive kiss
As the monitor
Reflects
No more.

Taking Your Place

Writing in lieu
Of killing the self
Heart halves
Break on the page

Pain writes
On dotted lines
Creating chapters
From what might
Have been

Fun and future
Join jilting
Feelings move
In rhythms
Memories loop
Through my head

Days pass
Nights drag
Pen and paper
Dare to touch
As I steel myself
To face
Whatever surfaces
Whatever remains

Sand

Crush these bones of belief
Into reality again
Sprinkle their remnants
      On the edge
      Of the ocean
      In the sand

Buff my Soul into sea glass
Into elegant remains
      Tucked into the pockets
      And buckets of a boy
      And a girl at play

On the beach
In the sun
      Reborn as a treasure
      Of unformed hopes
      Future jewels

Of a boy
And a girl
      At play

Trail of Tears

A trail of tears follows you like bread crumbs in a forest
Harmless remnants of the challenges you face

Most women can live through rapes and pillaging
Gathering together in righteous rage.

In the mist of a waterfall the sensitive one lives
Opening heart to heart like rainfall on a fragile limb

Sensitive one holds you, smudges your face, your chest
Takes you to the fire of initiation, into being a man
And whispers:

> Shed your skin great warrior
> Fear not the sword or the fire
> Weep your fears into the arms of midnight
> For morning still is here.

> Carry your mother to the water's edge
> Bathe her in your love and drown her with your anger
> Beat the sand into a bed of grief
>> Until you lay her down
>>> lay her down

> Drag your father to the mountaintop
> Carry him to the edge of the rim
> On a bed of pine needles burn your rage to the ground
> Love his bones as your bones
> Lift him up as you lift yourself
> Fill your bags with your pride, your fineness
>> And lay him down
>>> lay him down

Build a circle of juniper berries soaked in spirits
to bless the soul of your lost brother
Erect a teepee for your sister
Shelter her caring, her bitter dread

Heat the rocks
Drop them in
Sprinkle water
Drink it down
            Then lay it down
                lay it down

No more women need be dragged behind your horse
No more scalps or pants made of lovers' skin
No more tar baths reflected shiny black in the moonlight
Chiseling your form into a horrified stance

Take off your loincloth
Remove your chain vest
Unlock the shackles from your feet and hands
Rinse your lungs in the clarity of the warm stream
Touch your heart
            And lay it down
                lay it down

Saturday@Seven

I saw you

Walking

Hand in hand

With her

You had

A lilt

In your step

Is she

Victim

Or

Masterpiece

Neither

Yet knows

Scorpio #2, Easter egg hunt #37

A naturalist you say
as you press against
the next blond from a bottle.
Will she go gray in a couple of years
deferring to your wishes
bowing to your fears?

You're the prettiest girl I've ever been with

Okay…

Music and primal noises
were part of the plan.
Straight from the cookbook
of a semi-naked chef.

Uh-oh…

You let me in
like breath that can't be sucked back
into your braided heart
fighting to beat another lone day.

Stay away waves your flag
You kiss me and
Then you run away…
Run away run away run away…

Distraction?

May I offer you a distraction?
Cold glass, salt or no salt on that rim?

Perhaps a pretty girl with money
Or a sexy stranger without attitude

Distraction rocks as a strong prick talks
And waning dicks drink Cialis cocktails

Party on all you old fuckers
Denying rusted feelings for your mommies

Shut the door and strut some whore
Before your channel turns to 90.

Roll the dice and now bet twice
Hoping to win random satisfaction

Oh fuck it,
finally wake up
as a very large truck
filled with your stuff
rolls you fat and flat
under a big ole' heart attack

Lift your head a millimeter
To see one last peek at celebrity

As a hand reaches down
and a soft voice whispers
May I offer you a distraction?

Reflection from Him

Shame is so sweet
Cast across the room
onto the other side of the bed
like a rose in full bloom

Filters and mind frames turn
from my prick to her cunt
when unattractive feelings
enter my chest

Her breast
fails me
Her mind
bores me

As I close the window on love
reducing it to a fling
my satisfaction with myself returns

Lying flat on my pillow
I feel like a glorious fellow
until I rise and see
my own reflection in the glass.

My Body Combusts

Lying in the sun
Dreaming of another time
A time when I had you
With you around me
My body combusts
Burns away my loneliness
My body ignites
From oceans of desire

Lying in the sun
I see you in front of me
In the floaters
Crossing in my eyes
Washed with color
Blue and red—no gray

Lying in the sun
You come my way
In the hallucination
The elevation of your arms
Drawing me to you
I feel your breath
Smell your neck
You coolly carry me
As if I might break

Lying in the sun
You build a shade for me
Vowing protection
To never burn again
Sponging sweet orange water
Softly on my face
Ashes mix with sand
Breath flows from your kiss
Hearts beat into new form
Lying in the sun
My body combusts

Benediction

At the end of the day
Under the pain
Between two piles of ashes
Love remains

Saint Chapelle

Stained glass begs silence
To stand and raise a chalice
To you who admired this sacred place
Washed with beauty
Held together
Through centuries
By angels
Carved by hand
Gathered from land
Graced through wars
Unbroken
Mecca of meditative wonder
Complex color
Raises eyes
Bows heads
Invites prayers
For Souls passed
Hopes for future measure
Another century
S'il vous plait
An invitation to enter
Be still
To build up
Without tearing down
A place for our babies
To one day walk in
Sit down
Be silent
As the sunlight
Magnifies color
Over their skin
Through stained glass
Honed by the ages
Preserved
Just for them.

Arrested

Handcuffs clamp onto us
You at 13
Me at 3
Click, the sound seems
Inconsequential
As spirits fade

We do the dance
Of childhood
Pleasing, pleasing
Is our game

Too many presents
Wrapped with cruelty
Playing old songs
From memories
Of connection
Running to sit
On your lap
Slithering to escape

Beautiful place to die

You picked a beautiful place to do yourself in my friend
Past a desert golf course and a brand new city dump
Farm road 62, Forest road 24, down a deeply rutted road
Left before the second upright warning, marking cattle guards
(which would surely break a high-heeled shoe)
Left, then left again to a small mesa

There the full range of the Sangre de Christos continue to live
To expand with a huge thunderhead above blooming like a rose
Soft thunder muffled our moans as I laid flowers on the place,
the very place where your wild, sweet, funny ride came to an end.

Five friends trekked in a caravan to see this beautiful, awful place.
To bring chocolate and cigarettes and place rocks marking your action
that left heart breaks in friends who loved you so.
We told stories and laughed, feeding you tiny sips of beer.

The winds blew and a waxing moon rose before we left you there.
Our band of gypsies rocked away in four-wheel drives,
arms aching for another hug and a look into your azure blue eyes.
The horizon line turned pink to soften the turn into traffic, back into life.
There was nothing else to do.

Standing Sentry

I stand sentry
Eyes at attention
Waiting for you
To break down the door
Scream some more
Run to stand
Arms held high
Carrying a light
Protect me tonight

Walk through thorns
And great men
Sweat and stones
Ask now, begin
To wrap love
Body and soul
To bury all sorrows
Speed toward tomorrow
Plant a path
A rough draft
Live a pact
With no breaks
We push through
Standing sentry
In the center
Of our circle

Permission

Take a deep breath

Who sets
      permission
      into motion?

What force authors
      the ways we
      move around?

When love hits
      a brick wall
Stand back
      try again
Bathing in
      the idea

Relax and know

Love is everything.

A Cup of Tea

Steeped in grief
Like a bag of tea
Brewing in a fragile cup

Bands of death
Fly like a Stealth
Bombing my sense
Of reality

Lover, buddy,
friend and brother
Left through death
Or to find the other
Come back
I implore you

My soul consumed
By grief in my gut
Leave this sphere
Now proceed
I must

Sips of joy
Remembered friends
Comfort the blows
Calm my fears

Knowing memories
Will never leave
For now I hold
The key

To make a cup of tea
Steeping in my heart
I sit in wonder
That any of us
Found each other.

The Hug

Your arms wrapped
Me in a conversation
At first
Gestating in the rays
Of your eyes
So blue

Intermittent meetings
Rocked
Revealing parts
Of my life
To you

Organic orchestrations
Revealing manifestations
Of time
In here

Here, in this body
These cells
This memory
Experiences
Known only
To me
Now you

I giggled
At my brew of words
And you scooched
Back your chair
Reaching for my
Body to meet yours

Your hug
Embraced
A very soft
Sign

I felt your arms
Your neck
Until a chill inside
My breast
Began to press
Began to request
Release me
Please release me

I pulled away
You looked both ways
To see where stress
Interrupted
Your expression
Of peacefulness

I stayed aware and clear
Reciting oddly
Murmuring words
About fear

You looked puzzled
Leaned in
Listened
Wrapping a blanket
Of understanding
Around my foreign
Relationship
To hugs

Pushing and pulling
Truth tumbled through
Informing
Warming with innocence
And persistence
A strong desire to
Wake up
Be new

Scraping legs
On the floor
Your chair backed up
Your arms
Opened out
Embraced me
A careful hug
You heard

How odd it seemed
Man met revelation
Immediate action
Now what I really
Want to know
Will hugs shut down
While fear rolls around
And finds a place to go?

Or will peaceful
Pleasure abound
In subsets
Allowing trust
To grow

Surrender says,
"Who knows"?

Winter on Martha's Vineyard

Within this island
Salt air refines
Long held memories
Cold waves splash
Reality on my back
Defining distance
From you

This vineyard in winter
Replicates
The harsh environment
Drowning in frozen loss
Formed from you losing me

Inside a cabin
Walking on wood
Planks twice my age
I pad through rooms
Seeking a place to relax

On this table I write
Seven sealed letters
About what we forgot
Words come as evening
Bows to last light

In the bathtub
A lone candle
Illuminates a fading
Bouquet of hydrangea
I sip champagne
On the edge of a dream
Bathing in your touch

Winter on the vineyard
My feet in the drifts
Of sand and wind
Emotions implode
Creativity explodes
Bold in the sense
That no one really knows

Surrender

For a year I dug my garden with a begging spade
"Come back to me
Wake up—see me"
I moaned as I turned the soil

You grew onions and garlic
sprinkled black pepper around your lands
keeping spirits away
Dirt flew in great chunks
down the hill they rolled
down the hill rolling toward hell

I read and prayed from almanacs to scripture
"Please grant us a better day"
Your work truck sped up
my plow got stuck
as sunset after sunset faded to gray

Fears woke me
Erratic heartbeats assaulted your rest
The moon rose as I laid my head on your chest
"Rest well" whispered so quietly that only God could hear
Green eyes tear up, regret grips
as you realize no one is there to tell
In morning's light you yoke your oxen
and point them down the rows
plowing lines between rows of lavender
I planted long ago.

Down the hill I lie on a thin straw mat
In corpse pose I surrender—flat, on my back
My gaze drifts through branches of adolescent cherry trees
A small orchard approximating a much larger dream
You float above me, green eyes meet brown
Love grows from the roots of middle earth
Flowers, hard to see, bloom through sand

I blink, you're gone, flying like a ladybug working like a bee
while a steady praying mantis steps cautiously over me
I rise and roll my mat, a mantra takes your place
"Please deliver me to my greatest good"
I repeat from the shadow of your embrace

Red sweet cherries fill deep baskets as I chant my loving song
Yellow and red onions fill your great sacks, garlic overflows
And no one knows where the dirt will track
Or if pollen will land on our backs.

Moonrise

Sometimes when I see the moon rise in daylight
I wonder, can the sun also see heaven or hell
sitting on either side of me
or the romance of moon dust raining through pear trees
as Adam and Eve try again, once more,
to be in the garden, hold hands, immersed in joy
until morning when snakes crawl into their holes
and stars tack the universe together, hidden by the sun.

Sometimes when I see the moon rise in daylight
the world clears, and Venus glows her brightest.
The world is kissed with peace dreams
as Eden's garden sleeps.

Finding me

In the silence of the new moon
You will find me there
Naked in the tall grass
The river washes my hair
Wet skin dries from the breeze
My scent guides you
To where I lie in a circle of trees
The wind weaves through limbs
Needles cushion our bed
Passion surmounts separation
Forgiveness is our prayer
In our ceremony of karma
No one can explain
Why your eyes meet mine
And between the gaze
Our lives connect
Spirit whispers
Let love flow

Your tears of joy
Spin crystals
Glittering in starlight
Your arms surround me
Our dance can begin
As clouds move in time
Softening the dawn
Waking life-force
From dreams

Friend and lover
Choosing each other
Till the end
Choosing each other again

Sacrifice

If
I sacrifice
The rest of my life

Will
That make love
Real to you

Will
That knowledge
Of being loved

Soak
All the way
Into your skin

Fill
The hollow
Crevices

Scarred
From years
Of not knowing

Wondering
If you deserve
Connection that's real

Doubt
Drives your heart
Grasping and pushing
In tandem beats

Creating
Maddening
Chaotic passion
Numbing loneliness

Hiding
Then gliding
Magically funny
In the open
Closing inside
Thinking
No one sees
This pas de deux
As another night
Spins by

Motion
Covers emotion
Until guards fail

Loss
Creeps in
Shines through
A crack in the door
Where angels
Bring medals
Garnishing your life
Warm wings
Tether
Compassion
Sad reactions
Toward acceptance
Of being loved

Die dreaming
Even scheming
Escaping
Sacrifices
Negating love

Drifting on a Dream

Drifting on a memory
Out into the sea
Filled with the universe
Of you and me
Waves well up, then down
Searching for a schooner
A transport out of dust

Dolphins come to rescue
Our time on the salty sea
Lift us gently upon their backs
Swimming toward eternity
Spirit throws life preservers
Down through rays of sun

Oars of heart warriors
Fall together in time
Our hands reach out
Clasping passion
Swimming toward
A sacred place
A place to land

Beachy seaweed between our toes
The scent of torches fills this night
Wild orchids living to bloom
Friends stand near
Reciting their cheers
Lines encouraging
Our presence to claim

Strands of sea grass
Weave together
Coral as a canopy
Dancing in firelight
Love melts all fears

We are each person
Magnified through light
Cleansed by salt
And fed by water, by air
Reflected in the love of the other

Into the Rugged Frontier of Joy

Joy, she said,
As the consultation began
Quickly, I realized
We weren't discussing

Joy, the pretty blonde
Reading the New York Times
Cover to cover
Everyday at coffee

Or

Joy, my lovely aunt
Who can only sign
And smile and see

Or

Joy to the world
All the boys and girls
The happy refrain
Of an old song:
Jeremiah was a bullfrog
He was a good friend of mine

Not knowing a bull frog,
Serene beauty
Or the eternal silence of deafness
I wondered about joy…

Among glimmers of vivid reflections
My mind scans for highlights
Those moments above the trees
Where red-winged hawks form Zs
In the sky they fly
Hovering, spreading good medicine
From extended wings
Holding an anchor of joy in nature
Being free

Peaceful, my body
Rests in the joy
Of the rugged mountain
And the chilly springs

The movement of creation
Vibrates from the earth into my hands
Glowing like leaves in the wind
Blowing invitations to emulate
The stature of the mountains
To remain fluid like the streams

New Year's Silence

Falling into silence
In a chair
Sound of snow
Winter birds inch toward my toes

Full moon reflects
Thoughts inside me
Deer creep near nibbling fear
Noble, clustered in families

Eyes meet mine
Brown on brown
Echoing stillness
Trusting the place
They found me

Wind moves winter limbs
Snow settles down
Isolation surrounds me

A circle of stars
Stare in peace
Wishing me well
In my retreat
As I allow myself,
Some silence.

The Look of your Face

Ruddiness

Turns holy

Sun spots clear

Replaced

by floaters

As my eyes

Take in

Your skin

My hands

Touch

your chin

Beard

now white

Avoiding

By agreement

Meeting eyes

You raise

Your hat

Breaking

The shadow

Of my presence

On the edge

Of no memory

Naked symmetry

Designed

Through

The golden mean

Forehead

To chin

Everything

Between

Ears and fears

Your smile

Draws

Good-byes

From

The look

Of your face.

No To Self

I think of yoga
    a pose
    body
    nourished
by 10,000 years of practice

Instead I sit and stare
minutia in my head
Ideas scream at me
        paper
        pastels
beg for creation
a hundred manifestations
of I AM HERE
marked by an X
in a box
not to be forgot
grabbing color
brushing away tears
        I am here
        I am here
        I am here.

ACKNOWLEDGMENTS

*I want to list everyone who ever said "you're a good writer"
and with those words helped me to continue this life-long
process which has kept me some form of sane. So from Martha
and Mike McDonald through Sara Kennedy and Ross Moyer,
Jamie Baldwin, Kelly Michel, David and Ann Laser, John
Rochester, Beverly Barnett, Dana Waldon, Rebecca Skeele,
Sonya Haynie, Lisa Farrand, Ron Adinolfi, and Barbara Digby.
Thank you.*

*Thank you also to Karen Klinefelter who encouraged me to take
some time for myself. Thank you to Alix Bjorklund and Sharon
Stine for carefully listening. To Gary Grimm who waded
through oceans of tears with me, listened compassionately and
helped me realize that regardless of the subject or the title I was
always writing about myself. Thank you.*

*Kate Greenway served as the midwife of this book. She sat with
me in her yurt and stirred the metaphorical, magical urn which
helped me follow through with this book and continue to reveal.
Thank you, Kate.*

*Thank you to Dennis Jarrett who edited my work, praised me
and sent work to the trash. Through all of his careful comments
he never lost sight of this finished book.*

*David Chickey skillfully harnessed my vision into a book design.
I appreciate his experience, talents and generosity very much.*

*Thank you to my beautiful daughter, Natalie whose love I
don't ever have to doubt. Her presence in my life is as
important as the headwaters to a mountain stream.*

Published 2011 by **be bold books**

Copyright © 2011 by **Reese Taylor**

be bold books

www.reesetaylorpoetry.com

ISBN: 978–1–934435–34–2